# Common Sense Campaigning

## 5 BASICS TO CONSIDER WHEN PLANNING TO RUN FOR OFFICE

WRITTEN BY
## LAKESHA WOMACK
POLITICAL STRATEGY CONSULTANT
WOMACK CONSULTING GROUP



ISBN:9781975678678

*This book is dedicated to every person who has thought about running for office but didn't know where to start. I hope these BASICS give you a reference point so that when you're ready to jump out there, you have some ideas about who you will be as a candidate, what your staff will look like, how to recruit volunteers, who will vote for you, and what your campaign brand looks like.*

*I can't cover everything in this little guide so remember it's only a starting point. You need a team to win but you're the head of that team!*

*Lead with knowledge, excellence and integrity.*

# COMMON SENSE CAMPAIGNING

Common Sense isn't so common in politics.

I have worked on local, state, and federal campaigns in various capacities for almost twenty years. Campaigns who have large budgets typically fair better. Not because the candidate is usually that much better than their opponent but it is often the result of the candidate with the larger budget having access to more resources, being better organized, and operating more efficiently. Obviously, there are exceptions to the rule but most candidates who don't have experience or a team don't know what they don't know. This guide will not tell you everything that you need to know but hopefully, it will help you to think about some basics that you need to run a winning campaign.

# 5 Basics to Consider When Planning to Run for Office


COMMON SENSE CAMPAIGNING ............................................................4

THE CANDIDATE ............................................................................7

WHY ARE YOU RUNNING? ...............................................8

DO YOU HAVE ANY MONEY? .......................................... 10

DO YOU LIKE PEOPLE? ................................................. 12

DO YOU HAVE THE TIME TO DEDICATE TO A CAMPAIGN? ................... 15

CAN YOU FOLLOW DIRECTIONS? ..................................... 18

WHAT IS IMPORTANT TO YOU? ....................................... 22

WHAT IS IN YOUR PAST? .............................................. 25

WHO DO YOU KNOW THAT CAN HELP YOU? ......................... 28

WHAT CHANGES IF YOU WIN? ........................................ 30

WHAT CHANGES IF YOU LOSE? ...................................... 32

THE STAFF ..................................................................34

FINANCIAL MANAGEMENT ............................................. 48

MEDIA RELATIONS ..................................................... 52

STRENGTHENING YOUR TEAM ....................................... 57

THE VOLUNTEERS.............................................................59

DON'T WASTE PEOPLE'S TIME........................................ 60

SUPPLY THE BASICS.................................................... 62

Score bonus points. ............................................. 63

Create talking points. .......................................... 65

Leverage their networks. ....................................... 67

Listen! ....................................................... 69

**THE VOTER** ................................................ 71

Who are they? .................................................. 72

What is their voting history? ................................... 73

Why would they support you? .................................... 77

What makes you different from your opponent(s)? ........... 79

How many voters do you need to win? ...................... 81

How will you get them to come out and vote? ..................... 85

**THE CAMPAIGN** ............................................. 90

Branding ....................................................... 91

Look like a winner ............................................. 93

Using online tools ............................................. 95

Direct Mail .................................................... 101

Location ....................................................... 104

Messaging ...................................................... 106

Fundraising .................................................... 108

**ABOUT THE AUTHOR** ......................................... 110

LaKesha Womack ................................................. 110

# THE CANDIDATE

Congratulations on considering a run for political office. I cannot image that it has been an easy decision to make and you might not even be fully committed but I applaud you for opening yourself to the possibility. It is important for you to think very seriously about who you are, who you want the public to know you as, and which values are most important for you to hold on to. We will discuss the campaign last because I believe there are some other issues that you need to give serious consideration to because they will help to formulate your campaign strategy, branding, and messaging.

# Why are you running?

The most important question that you need to ask yourself is, **why am I running?**

There are going to be many days when this is going to get hard, you're going to feel like giving up, and people are going to tell you to give up. On those days, you will need to reflect on your why.

Why are you doing this?

Do you have an earnest desire to help your community?

Did something happen to propel you to make this decision? What is it?

The worst reason to run is because someone prompted you or paid you to do it. We have enough useless elected officials destroying our democracy, don't become of them. Legislating is about more than sound bites and collecting a check. There are people who are counting on the decisions that you will make to maintain or better their lives. No matter how insignificant you may think the position is today, it will have some ripple effect on someone's life tomorrow.

Additionally, you need to consider the long-term effects of the decisions you will make. Politicians can be short sighted at times and only see what is directly in front of them but your decisions, your words, your actions may carry on for generations into the future.

**Why are you running?**

# Do you have any money?

Campaigns are not cheap.  Maybe if you are running for a local position with no opposition. Everyone else needs to think about how you're going to finance this operation.

Are you going to use personal resources?

Are you going to fundraise?

Are you going to connect with PACs (Political Action Committees)?

As you are thinking about these resources, you need to consult the FEC (Federal Elections Commission) and your state elections commission to gain an understanding of the rules around campaign finances. I don't want to see anyone going to jail for violating campaign finance laws on a state or federal level. Of course, there are consultants and financial experts that you can hire to manage the process but you still need to have a clear understanding of the rules for yourself because ultimately YOU will be held accountable for the actions of your campaign.

Understanding the laws is the first step, deciding which resources you will use to build your stash is next but you also need to start thinking about how you will need to spend the money. Campaign financing is very unpredictable. As you are considering your budget, you need to plan through Election Day with a monthly or milestone break down as

well as priorities for your spending - what are the necessities and what are the wants. Always cover the necessities and make sure you are prepared for the necessities at the next milestone or for the next month before spending on the wants.

Right now, you should start thinking of a number that you can commit to. We will discuss your campaign budget in more detail later.

# Do you like people?

I know this sounds like a silly question but...

**Do you like people?**

For real?

Campaigning is going to require you to be around a lot of people. It's going to require you to sometimes put their needs before your own.  It's even going to require you to think about what's important to them instead of what's important to you. One of the failures of our current political system is that too many elected officials are operating in their own self-interest.

How often do they really take a poll of their constituents to gain an understanding of how they feel about issues and then act accordingly?

Go ahead and think about it. It doesn't happen often enough. Even when they hold "town halls," it is to allow people to air their grievances but they rarely come with an open mind, willing to be challenged and possibly change their stance based on the desires of their constituents. If you want to represent the people, you need to like them, in fact you may even consider loving them because love often remains when we don't like people very much.

Additionally, campaigning will require you to knock on the doors of strangers and to call people who you have never met. You need to be able to do these things with joy in your heart, an earnest desire to make a connection with these people and possibly ask them for money in addition to their vote. That's a tall ask if your starting point is not liking people.

Some candidates are not a fan of the people but they love the political process. They love the power that comes from making important decisions. That's great but you should always remember that those decision affect people.

Most of your decisions will have some effect on the persons who voted for you or who you are hoping to vote for you. Don't get so caught up in the political process and intoxicated by the political power that you forget about the people.

# Do you have the time to dedicate to a campaign?

One of the biggest mistakes that I have seen candidates make is not creating time to campaign. It's like they assume that they don't have to work for votes. Let me tell you, voters want you to ask for their vote and to work for their vote. They may say they are tired of the door knocks and phone calls but I guarantee you if their neighbor gets a door knock or a phone call and they don't, they will have major issues. You need to look at your calendar and figure out how much time can you realistically dedicate to campaigning between your announcement day and Election Day.

*Hint... just blocking off Saturdays will not be enough.*

How much time your campaign will require is going to depend on the geographic size of your area, the number of voters in your area, and the amount of time you have until Election Day. Obviously, a local race will require less time but don't think that less equals none. People still want to see you and they want to hear from you. They want to know that you want the position, why you want it, and how you plan to use it to help them.

One of the ways that you can maximize your campaign time is to ask residents to host events and to invite their neighbors. Make sure that they understand that you can only stay for a short amount of time but give them the opportunity to meet you in a more personal setting. This will give them the feel of really getting to know you.

Also, it will give you a chance to speak directly to their issues when asking for their support. If there are issues that you are not aware of, don't know how they fit into your platform, or don't know if they will fall into your office's

Also, it will give you a chance to speak directly jurisdiction; be honest with the people. Tell them you will find out and make it a priority to follow up. People would rather hear the truth, even if they don't think so at the moment. A lie that will follow your reputation longer than a follow up.

# Can you follow directions?

Most candidates foolishly believe that they are in charge.  You're not. At every step, you will be receiving requests, directions, invitations, and demands. You need to figure out how well you follow directions and how well you can negotiate compromises.

I believe that everyone who approaches candidates to help them wants something. So many candidates find themselves blindsided because they think people are naturally good and want to give their time and money to you because they really believe in you. Not in this lifetime. You need to develop the ability to ask very plainly, what do you need from me? Be prepared for anything to follow that question.  Also, be prepared to stand on your integrity when providing an answer.

There will be some requests that will make your stomach turn. No matter how big the check, say no. You may think that no one will ever find out but you end up being held hostage to this "secret" and that can feel like a black cloud hovering over you every time you meet people.

There will be some requests that will make your brow furrow because you're not sure how you should respond, say let me get back to you. Filter the request through an adviser or your Campaign Manager and trust their opinion.

And there will be some requests that will feel like a no brainer, say we can work on that. Never promise more than you are certain you can deliver and as a candidate, there is nothing that you are certain you can deliver except your integrity and the desire to work in the best interest of your constituents.

Back to following directions...

So, you have all of these people pulling at you while you're dedicating time and money to try to get elected... this requires discipline and a Campaign Manager. If you don't hire any other position, you need a Campaign Manager so that you have someone to filter all your thoughts, invitations, and deliberations through. You need someone who you can trust to be honest with you and someone who you can be honest with. Campaigning is a lonely road to travel because you will find that everyone wants something.

There will be moments when you will feel like you have nothing left to give. Your Campaign Manager should be the one person whose directions you will follow because you know they have your best interest at heart. They can help you to see how things that are being done today will work toward the goal of getting you elected. This person's integrity should match your own because when those questionable situations arise, this is the person who you should rely on to help you think through how this will not only affect the campaign but how this will affect your reputation in the long term.

# What is important to you?

Underneath the statement of, "why am I running," needs to be a list of the five values that are most important to you. These values will help you to remember who you are at the core. They will serve as your moral compass.

I wish I could tell you that politicians aren't corrupt. I wish I could guarantee you that you won't become corrupt. I wish I could tell you that corrupt politicians are bad people. Most of them are not. I don't think anyone ever goes into politics aspiring to be corrupt but one questionable decision makes it easier to make the next questionable decision and before you know it, you have ventured away from your moral compass. Remembering your core values, who you were before the campaign and why you're doing this should be the foundation that you stand on every day.

Unless you are running as an Independent, you will likely be affiliated with a political party. That party has a set of "values" that they aspire to demonstrate through drafting legislation and voting. Do not become so consumed with the values of a party that you forget the values of the people who have placed their faith in your ability to stand up for them in spaces that they may never have access to. You are asking to lead all the people in your area, not just those in your party, not just those who like you, not even the ones who voted for you but every single person in your area lives in this thing called a democracy where we believe that our vote is our voice. Even if our candidate loses, we expect the person who wins to look out for us.

Your core values should allow you to uphold those principles. Even when you must stand alone, if you are standing with your constituents, you have them behind you but most importantly, you are able to go to sleep

at night knowing that your values have not
been compromised.

# What is in your past?

No one is perfect. Let's start here. I doubt very seriously that you have never done anything wrong. If you haven't then you're kinda lame (just kidding but not really) and lying to yourself.  People like candidates that they can relate to but... we need to understand how relatable you should be.

First, make a list of all the people who know about the questionable decisions that you've made in the past. What are the chances that once you announce they will suddenly develop a desire to share those fond memories? You think it won't happen but rest assured, it may and you will need to be prepared. I am amazed at how many pictures from my college party days pop up on my Facebook timeline when I start posting about political issues. It is almost like there are people who want to remind me of my past. Luckily, I decided a long time ago to own whatever mistakes I made in the past. After all, I didn't murder anyone and the statute of limitations have passed for any other offenses that I know of.

Next, think about the actions. In our minds, our indiscretions often feel like the worst things in the world but get real for a minute... will anyone really care?

Did you smoke pot? No one cares.

Did you try cocaine? A few may care but own it and chalk it up to a rough phase in your past.

Did you cheat on your spouse? Are you still together? You worked it out and are stronger because of it. Did you separate? It's a painful and private event in your past.

You need to be prepared for whatever could come up. There's a huge chance that it won't but be prepared for anything.

Think about these situations, the people who may have been involved, and the spin you will place on the incident if it should come up.

Yes, I said it.

You need to understand how spin works and if you don't understand, find someone who does to help you. Spin is not lying. Do not be a lying spinner. People hate lies and they really hate lies that are disguised as spin. Spin is taking a story and finding the (truthful) angle that you want to use to tell that story and sticking to it. Always stick to your story - don't offer extra information to make it believable. Keep it simple.

# Who do you know that can help you?

By now, you're probably thinking that this is a lot to tackle and we haven't even started talking about the campaign.

So, who can help you?

Yes, family members are great but who do you know with some political campaign experience that can help you?

Do you know someone who has run for a political office before?

Can your local political party help?

Are there any political training seminars that you can attend?

This is not an endeavor that you want to embark on by yourself unless it is a local race and you are running unopposed. Everyone else should start researching resources that can help you. As you are working through this guide, think about your strengths – the things that you can easily accomplish by yourself. Next think about your weaknesses - the areas where you know you need help.

Getting help is not a sign of weaknesses. It shows that you are smart enough to know what you don't know and wise enough to find the people who do know so they can help you.

The biggest fool is the one who only considers his own advice.

# What changes if you win?

So much effort is placed on getting to the finish line that many people don't honestly consider how their life will change if they win.

What is the time commitment that will be involved with your new position?

What is the travel commitment?

Is there is any training required before you step into the position?

Are there any skills that you need to brush up on?

Begin your campaign with the end in mind. It may be hard to believe but you I know of people who have campaigned for and won positions that are considered full time jobs but they had no plan to quit the full time job that they had before the campaign. Unless you plan to work two full time jobs, you need to have an exit strategy prepared to execute upon winning. No one will want to hear excuses about why you cannot perform the duties that you have campaigned to perform.

You should also prepare your family members for the changes that might be coming your way. Some things that you do with your family and friends may not be in your best interest to continue doing publicly. No, it's not fair but as an elected public official, you need to consider your image as a community leader. Remember, this is a part of the package that you are asking for.

*For clarification... this does not mean that I am telling you to start acting like you are the winner but it absolutely means that you need to have a plan for life after winning.*

# What changes if you lose?

There is a possibility that will not be victorious on Election Day. I hate being the one to say that but it's true.

The bad news will be that you will feel like you spent all this time and money for nothing.

You may cry. It's ok, just don't do it in front of any media.

You may scream and curse because you can't believe you lost to "that" person. It's ok, just don't do it in front of any media.

The good news can be that you developed a community of likeminded people who can support you in your next endeavor.

You need to plan and work each day with the expectation that you will be victorious. You can't campaign thinking about losing. You must leave it all on the field and treat every campaign day like it is the two minute warning in the fourth quarter of the Super Bowl.

Whether you win or lose, you should know
that you didn't leave any stone unturned.

# THE STAFF

One of the biggest, well two of the biggest mistakes that candidates make are

1) thinking they can do it all by themselves and

2) thinking they can do it all with volunteers.

You need at least one person that you are paying to be on your team because you can't dictate the comings and goings of volunteers. It doesn't matter what they say ok to in an interview, what you make them sign, or how dedicated they say they are to you and/or your cause. You need a paid staffer whose day to day job is overseeing your campaign activities.

Just like with any other job, you should be realistic about the expectations of your staff, otherwise you will have a high turnover. Your staff members will take their positions as seriously as you take them. If you have a very

relaxed and casual attitude then they will
model that but if you are punctual and
professional then you should expect them to
model that.

# Paid Positions

Most of the staff positions that I will list below will require dedication and possibly long hours. These are not positions that you should expect people to volunteer for, however some of the positions can be independent contractors instead of full time staff members. If you choose to use independent contractors, you should consider having contracts that stipulate whether they can work with other candidates while working on your campaign and have them sign nondisclosure agreements.

If you are serious about winning this election, you need to work with people who have some experience working on a campaign. Depending on your budget and race, you may not be able to afford someone with a lot of experience. You can consider hiring recent college graduates who have the education but little to no experience. Be careful about placing these persons in positions that require them to oversee developing your campaign strategy. I have nothing against recent college grads but most of their knowledge is theoretical. You want some of them in the room because they may help you connect your strategy with a younger audience and they may be aware of more recent trends than someone who has been working primarily in the field. However, they often lack the inherent knowledge that comes from working directly with voters. You may get lucky and find the purple unicorn who has been gaining experience while in college. You want that person.

Based on the following descriptions, prioritize the needs for your campaign. For each position, attempt to interview at least three candidates. To find candidates, contact your local or state party. They often have a database of campaign staffers looking for their next election. You can also find a training program in your area and ask them to recommend persons.

Before you pull the "you're hired" trigger, make sure you have the funds to pay the staffer(s), a clear description of what you want them to do, the estimated time commitment, benefits (if you have any), the required employment paperwork prepared and policies and procedures including a confidentiality/non-disclosure agreement.

# Chief of Staff

The Chief of Staff is responsible for maintaining the campaign headquarters, coordinating the administrative aspects of the campaign, the hiring and management of staff and creating and managing the campaign budget. They work closely with the Field Directors to identify, recruit and manage volunteers to help with various campaign activities. This person needs to have a good overview of the entire campaign, the ability to solve problems as they arise, strong interpersonal skills, patience, persistence, enthusiasm, good communication skills and the ability to work with all kinds of people.

Salary Range: $3,000-$5,000 per month

# Campaign Manager

The campaign manager oversees the day-to-day operations of the campaign, the coordination and implementation of the fundraising operations and ongoing coordination with the candidate. They also work with specific constituency groups to organize their involvement with the campaign. They develop a voter contact plan in coordination with the field directors for particular communities by building relationships with the existing organizations that represent these communities. Campaign managers must have excellent organizational skills, be level headed, have good interpersonal skills and not be afraid of raising money.

Salary Range: $3,000-$5,000 per month

# Finance Director

The finance director oversees the financial and accounting aspects of the campaign. They monitor all contributions, maintain financial records and are responsible for compliance with the relevant election board. The finance director approves and monitors the budget. They must have significant experience in accounting or finance.

Salary Range: $1,000-$2,000 per month

# Deputy Finance Director

The deputy finance director is responsible for raising the money that will allow the campaign to accomplish its goals. The deputy finance director works closely with the candidate, campaign manager, finance director and finance committee to meet the financial goals of the campaign. They oversee keeping the candidate on track with fundraising, preparing for and staffing call time and overseeing all fundraising events. A good fundraiser must be highly organized, outgoing and willing to push the candidate and campaign toward meeting their fundraising goals.

Salary Range: $2,000-$4,000 per month

# Press Secretary

The press secretary oversees all the campaign's interactions with the media. They build relationships with the press, communicate with the media as the key spokesperson, set up interviews, identify media opportunities for the campaign and manage the social media platforms for the candidate. They may help write and develop campaign literature, draft speeches for the candidate and create copy for the campaign website. The press secretary should have prior experience and contacts with the media, be a good writer and communicator and be a proactive thinker and strategist.

Salary Range: $2,000-$4,000 per month

# Field Directors

The field directors oversee making sure the campaign gets its message out through direct voter contact. Their main responsibility is to develop a comprehensive plan for their area that includes door knocking and phoning to identify voters and persuade them about the candidate. They may also coordinate voter registration efforts. Finally, they coordinate the GOTV effort. The field directors need to be visible in their community, highly organized, energetic, capable of motivating and managing volunteers and able to manage large quantities of data. Field directors should have specific territories that they are responsible for.

Salary Range: $2,000-$3,000 per month (each)

# Scheduler

The scheduler is responsible for accepting and acting on all invitations, seeking out potential events and putting together the candidate's schedule. The scheduler makes sure the candidate, campaign manager and chief of staff are briefed about each of the events and is given proper directions, contact information and collects briefing information from the other team members on each event. The scheduler also ensures that the candidate call-time and voter contact time remains the top priority. The scheduler needs to be assertive, meticulous with details, pleasant on the phone and able to say "no" when necessary.

Salary Range: $2,000-$4,000 per month

# Technology Manager

The information technology manager coordinates and manages all aspects of the campaign regarding the technology – website, database, etc. The technology manager's responsibilities range from maintaining the website to developing the database to providing a computer network for the staff. The technology manager is responsible for securing phones and computers with the necessary technology for all paid staff members, developing the voter database and providing a computer network for the staff. This person needs to have a broad knowledge of technology, computers and software and can work in a rapid paced environment.

Salary Range: $1,000-$2,000 per month

# Legal and Compliance Advisor

The legal advisor should be versed in all aspects of election law and campaign finance.

Salary Range: $1,000-$2,000 per month

# Financial Management

I cannot stress the importance of following campaign finance rules. It may seem trivial because you are involved in a small race. It may be something that you think you can outsource. However, there is no excuse for you not to visit the FEC and Secretary of State websites to determine which campaign finance laws pertain to your campaign. Do not rely solely on the opinions of others for this information.

Once you understand the rules, you need to designate someone to operate as your Treasurer and/or Finance Director. Ideally, this person will also be familiar with state and federal campaign finance laws. Some states will require this person to undergo additional training as well as hold them accountable for all your filings.

When designating a person, make sure you both understand their responsibilities. You will need to meet with this person and your Campaign Manager on a regular basis, at least once per week, to discuss the status of your campaign and your finances.

You may have a person in charge of fundraising but ultimately, it is up to you to bring money into the campaign. After all, people are investing in you, your vision and your platform.

Once you determine how much you need, you need to have a strategy to help you generate those funds. *Hint... asking people for money should be one of them.* If you're not comfortable asking people to contribute to your campaign then you need to start practicing. Always ask for and plan to raise more than you need.

Some examples of expenses to consider (amounts will depend on your timeframe, geographic location, and opponents):

# Administration

- ❖ Staff
- ❖ Health Care
- ❖ Payroll Tax
- ❖ Headquarters and Utilities
- ❖ Phones and Internet
- ❖ Office Supplies
- ❖ Candidate Travel and Expenses
- ❖ Computers and Technology

# Fundraising

- ❖ Letterhead and Envelops
- ❖ Postage
- ❖ Credit Card Fees
- ❖ Email List serve

# Polling and Research

- ❖ Self Research
- ❖ Opposition Research
- ❖ Focus Groups
- ❖ Benchmark Polls
- ❖ Tracking Polls

# Communications

- ❖ TV ads
- ❖ Radio ads
- ❖ Direct Mail
- ❖ Social Media ads
- ❖ Website design, hosting and maintenance
- ❖ Cyber security
- ❖ Marketing collateral
- ❖ Swag

# Voter Turnout

- ❖ Voter files
- ❖ Yard signs
- ❖ Office food
- ❖ Election Day expenses

# Media Relations

**Every candidate wants good press.** It's a fact that we as humans like to hear good things being said about us. Unfortunately, campaigns are often breeding grounds for negative news. Everyone wants to know what's wrong with you instead of why you will be the perfect person to serve.

Sad?

I know. But that's why you need a strategy to work with the media. That involves creating the story about you and your campaign that you want them to focus on. Having a press kit on your website that includes links to your press releases, approved images, a professional bio, and a summary of your campaign platform will decrease the likeliness (not prevent) that a journalist will need to dig up information about you.

**Plan for the best but prepare for the worst.** Remember when we discussed mistakes in your past? Well, you need to have a file saved on your computer (not in the cloud) with your stories planned in case any of those incidents become public. Depending on the nature of your political race, your opponents may be doing opposition research to dig up dirt on you (and you will probably do opposition research on them). There is a chance that something from your past will come out but it probably won't come from the other campaign. It will come through the media. If your opponent's find something that they consider juicy, they will more than likely pass it along to the media and if the media considers it "newsworthy" or something the voters need to know, they will reach out to you for a comment. This is when you pull out that little file and run with your statement. Make sure it's TRUE. No matter how you must spin the truth, do it but don't lie. Once you get caught in a lie, your credibility starts to diminish. People will forgive an admitted cheating, crackhead who apologizes quicker than they will forget someone who lied.

**Stay informed.** You should watch the news and read the news headlines every day and be prepared to comment on whatever the hot topic is for the news cycle. If you don't know or don't have an opinion that fits with your campaign platform - "no comment" or "let me get back to you on that" should be your go to responses. Don't make stuff up or say what you think they want to hear. Some of the most successful candidates win because of their discipline and their ability to stay on message.

**Censor yourself.** Refrain from making any off-color comments no matter how exclusive the crowd, how few people are in attendance, or how close you are with the person. And don't send it by email. In the age of social media, nothing is private. Even information in a private account or closed group can be shared through the magic of screen shots. Do not think that it will not happen to you. The people who you think are rooting for you can often be the ones orchestrating your demise. Always comment with caution.

What are some ways that you can generate press?

- Publish editorials in your local newspaper

- Host a press conference - when you announce, around a major event or when you have something newsworthy to share

- Send your media kit to the local television news stations. They may contact you when they need a quote on an upcoming story. Include your professional biography so they can see you as more than just a political candidate.

- Attend local charity events to show which issues you are compassionate about

# Strengthening Your Team

Your team members will essentially be your brand ambassadors. Whatever people think of them will be transferred to your campaign. You want to be sure that you are providing the training that they need to be successful. If you see an area that needs improving, don't hope and pray that it changes. Be proactive and take the necessary steps to provide the training and resources needed.

If you see there are issues between staff members, don't wait for it to blow over. Bring in all parties involved, at the same time, and mediate the situation. Being a leader requires that you be decisive and that you act. If you can't control your own campaign, it will send a clear signal about your ability to govern.

If your team rarely meets in person, consider hosting a lunch with them so that they have a chance to interact with each other. If you find that they are always together, find ways for them to work independently so they don't start getting on each other's nerves.

Most importantly, ensure they have time for self-care. Whether it's doing laundry, getting a haircut or visiting family; realize that these people have lives beyond the campaign. Some may be so committed to your campaign until they will not want to take time away but the time will give them a refreshed perspective and hopefully they will come back to work energized.

*Note: Once you are four weeks from Election Day, there are NO days off. Set this expectation at the beginning.*

# THE VOLUNTEERS

Volunteers are one of the hottest commodities in the campaign world. Most people who volunteer consistently for campaigns are extremely committed to the cause. Political volunteering is not something that many people just wake up and consider doing. Therefore, you need to treat your volunteers like the gold mines that they are. Dig deep to find the ones who are committed and will stick with you until the end but don't get upset if you have a high rate of turnover. There are a few people who will sign up and not show, some will show up one time and disappear off the face of the earth but if you treat the ones who stay well, your volunteers can become one of your most valuable assets.

# Don't waste people's time.

Campaigns are always seeking volunteers. My first question is - what do you want them to do?

Seriously, what tasks do you have available?

How long will it take to complete the task?

How many people are needed for each task?

When does the task need to be complete?

How does it help the campaign?

Before recruiting one volunteer, think about these things so that when the volunteers arrive, you are prepared for them. One of the worst looks for a campaign is to get people excited about getting involved then failing to contact them because there is no formal schedule or contacting them with nothing to do. No campaign can afford a bad volunteer experience because volunteers are also community ambassadors. They contribute to the community's assessment of your campaign.

# Supply the basics.

When asking volunteers to come and perform tasks, make sure you are providing the basics that they need to complete the tasks. Don't expect people to use their own phones to make calls for your campaign. Don't expect people to use their own printer, ink and paper to make copies for your campaign. You can ask people if they want to donate those items to the campaign office but everything a volunteer needs should be supplied, before they arrive.

Work with your staff to think through a volunteer's experience from the moment that they sign in until they leave. Based on the experience that you imagine, how likely are they to come back?

# Score bonus points.

Volunteers and supporters love swag! There are many studies that show that swag does not translate into votes. That may be true but let me say it again - volunteers and supporters love swag!

You need to allocate a percentage of your budget to yard signs, buttons, tee shirts, coffee mugs, pens, etc.  However, you need to be smart about how you distribute it.

For example, you can give a free tee shirt to anyone who donates over $100 and a shirt and coffee mug for donations over $250.  Make sure you buy quality products (preferably made in America) but not expensive. Make sure someone manages this system so that it is consistent.

For volunteers, you can give them rewards for each shift that they complete. For every two hours that they volunteer, they can pick one item out of the swag bag.  You can have a higher end swag bag for your volunteer leaders so that they see some benefit to the extra time and responsibility.

You may see this stuff as useless or a waste of money but it is branding. If you have designed the products to include your campaign slogan, logo and website, everywhere that your volunteers and supporters go with their swag, they are taking your campaign with them. Many consumers make buying decisions based on the reputation of a product and/or the recommendation from a friend. Many voters also cast ballots based on name recognition. You want your brand ambassadors generating name recognition for you everywhere that they go.

# Create talking points.

When you bring people on board, make sure they know who you are, why you're running, what your position does/will do, and that they understand your platform. These people will be making phone calls and knocking on doors for you. They should understand your campaign almost as well as you do. Every volunteer should receive some training about what they are being asked to do before they begin the task and a quick refresher at the beginning of each subsequent shift. Don't assume because someone had previous campaign volunteer experience that they know what you want to be done and how you want it done. Having a staff person to take the time to get the volunteers trained will show them that they are valuable to the work you are trying to do and not being used solely for free labor.

Make sure your talking points are plastered
around the campaign office, printed on sheets
for them to take with them, and integrated
into the scripts you provide them. Repetition is
the key to remembering. You want them to
not only remember your story but to repeat it.

# Leverage their networks.

Provide them with information to share on their social media networks. If they are members of the community, they are likely going to be connected with other members of the community. They may even be connected to people you haven't reached or aren't able to reach.

But... you need to have some control over what they are sharing so create share sheets for volunteer events with information about what they're doing, your social media usernames so they can tag you and a hashtag so you can see what they are saying. You should have someone in charge of monitoring your social media and that person should be checking what is being said about you, your campaign and your opponent every day. Nothing should come to you as a surprise.

This is also a great way to flag volunteers who may be working for the opposition but coming to your camp to get information. Trust people until they give you a reason not to trust them.

# Listen!

Your volunteers are your brand ambassadors and people will probably tell them things that they won't tell you or your staff. Encourage them to share that information with you. Even if it's something you don't want to hear, you need to hear it. It gives you a chance to turn negatives into positives or to clear up information that may be floating around and isn't true. So many candidates discount the influence that volunteers can have on a race. Your volunteers are great for helping you to get tasks accomplished but one of their greatest values is being a focus group in the community. They can tell you what people are really thinking about the issues in ways that polls may miss.

Having volunteers from all your demographics will also give you differing views of how the issues are being discussed. You may find that everyone supports developing land in a particular area but different groups have different ideas of what the land should be used for. By listening informally to the different ideas, you can take their ideas and find something everyone can agree upon.

# THE VOTER

Everyone in your area (legal and over 18) is a voter but not everyone in your area is your voter. It's important to understand that there are some people that you will never win over because your values/issues don't line up with theirs.

The good news: you don't need every voter to vote for you

The bad news: you need to know how many of the likely voters will probably turn out to vote and how many will likely vote for you (that number isn't usually known until election night even though there are some political strategists who can predict the number within the margin of error)

# Who are they?

Voter demographics can differ depending on the type of election. Is this a special election, primary, general or midterm? Your Secretary of State should have data about the voters in all the previous elections. When analyzing the data, look back to the previous three to five elections of the same type. Don't compare midterm election results to primary general election results. You need to compare apples with apples to determine how many likely voters you are expecting, which parties they represent and what the voter turnout is for the differing voting precincts.

# What is their voting history?

How did the voters vote?

How many voted for each party and for independents in each election?

How many registered voters didn't vote?

Can you see a pattern regarding the race of voters? Their age? Their gender?

Understanding these numbers will help you to determine where to focus your energy. Those who are already voting need to be convinced to vote for you. The groups with low voter turnout rates need to be persuaded to vote AND to vote for you.

Using data to determine those numbers will help you to be strategic with your messaging, which events to make a priority to attend, and which groups to solicit for extra volunteers. If there is a low voter turnout among the 18-25 demographic, you should consider hosting events and purchasing advertising that speaks to this group about getting out to vote for you. If you have a strong 50-65 base, send them direct mail to introduce yourself and your platform with a call to action for their vote. Don't waste money encouraging them to go vote if that's something they are already planning to do. Spend your resources on the behavior that you need to influence.

# What are the district's demographics?

As you are analyzing your voter data, also consider the demographics of your area.

- ✓ What is the median household income?
- ✓ Net worth?
- ✓ Home value?
- ✓ Is it a blue collar or white-collar area?
- ✓ What is the racial makeup?
- ✓ What is the age breakdown?
- ✓ Where do they work?
- ✓ What are most people doing on the weekend?

Understanding who your people are will help you to determine which issues they are more likely to care about, the best way to discuss those issues, and where to have those discussions. People often make assumptions about the needs of the community without taking the time to learn about the people they are seeking to represent.

I have worked with clients who have imagined their district's demographics to look one way and once they analyzed the data, they were shocked to see the makeup of the area. It helped us to determine what type of media to use, whether formal language or informal language would be most effective and which events would be a priority for the candidate to attend.

# Why would they support you?

Now that you know your community, why should those people give **you** their vote?

What's so special about you that they should think you have the answer?

This should form the basis of your stump speech. Speak to the people about their issues in a language that they understand. Lay out the problem, how your office should be solving it, and how you will make a difference.

Be realistic!

Don't stand up saying you're going to do things that you know you can't accomplish. Share your ideas and not your plans. Help them to understand the hierarchy of your position, how changes occur, and who else would need to be involved to create the change they are seeking.

Too often, we assume that people understand how the local, state, and federal government operates. There are people who have been voting all their lives but have no idea what the persons occupying the positions do nor do they understand how it affects their day to day lives. Make it plain so that people can connect the dots.

# What makes you different from your opponent(s)?

People are going to ask why they should choose you over the competition and you need to be prepared with an answer. Your answer should not highlight any negatives of your opponent(s) or even mention their name. However, it should be a statement that provides a clear compare and contrast to demonstrate where each of you stands and why your position is better for the community. If you have more than one opponent, start with "even though my opponents believe x, y and z; I believe..." and then go in to your platform.

State enough about your opponents to demonstrate that you are aware of the competing ideas but emphasize why your idea is better. You do not want to get caught in a back and forth with your opponents. Media and voter attention is hard to earn so you want to keep the focus on your platform.

# How many voters do you need to win?

One of the most important numbers for you to calculate is your vote number. How many votes do you need to win? This is not a concrete number but an estimate. You should plan to compile these numbers from the past three elections and use the average of those three elections.

Start with how many registered voters are in your area? Although all of these persons will not come out to vote, you need to see the trends in registrations. Think about how they compare with the area's number of citizens over the age of 18.

Is there a large group of people not registered to vote or are most of the citizens registered? This will help you to determine if you need to focus on voter registration, education/persuasion or both.

Next, look at the voter turnout. Of those registered, how many turned out to cast a vote? If there was an election with a much higher or lower voter turnout percent, you should have a staffer take a deeper look at the dynamics of that race.

Was there a hot issue?

Did one of the candidates have a strong GOTV effort?

Were there no issues that the voters resonated with?

Based on the turnout percentage, you may be able to see how influencing an additional five to ten percent of registered voters to come out and vote could have an impact on your race.

Next, you need to determine how many votes were cast for each party. This can be great news or challenging depending on which party you are representing. If you are running as an independent candidate, these numbers may be more challenging because in most areas, the majority of the votes are cast for one of the two major political parties. Do not be discouraged but realize that you will have to focus on voter registration to build your base, voter education to help voters understand who you are and what you stand for and voter persuasion to convince them to vote for you. Candidates associated with a political party typically only have to focus on two of those three.

Now that you have your numbers, let's look at them. In a perfect world, you would only need 51% of the voters on your side to declare victory. Well, it's not that easy and to get an exact calculation as well as demographic and precinct breakdown, you need to work with a political strategist.

To get a general idea, take the average of the voter turnout in the past three election cycles and multiply by 60%. I know you only need to 51% to win and possibly less than that depending on how many others are running but you can only focus on your race and it never hurt anyone to have too many votes.

Next, compare that number with the number of persons from your party that voted. Do you need more members of your party to get out and vote? Do you have enough members of your party voting to get you elected? If so, your primary focus should be ensuring that they get out and vote for YOU. The difference in votes needed and voters that can come from base will be the number of people that you need to register to vote or persuade from nonvoters, the other party or new voters to vote for you.

# How will you get them to come out and vote?

You can do everything right leading to Election Day and lose if you don't get people out to vote. It happens more than you know. Candidates believe all the people who say they're going to vote for them so they sit back and relax on Election Day.

Big mistake!

All your efforts should be building up to Election Day.

# Voter registration and education

Do you have enough likely voters in your area? If not, you may need to get some people registered. You should be looking for people who are new to the area and people who have just reached the age to vote. Don't stop at registering them, provide them with information about your platform and ask if they want to volunteer. So often we register people but we don't give them a compelling reason to cast a vote. Connect the issues to their personal situation. Teach your volunteers to do the same.

*Be mindful of your state's rules about registering voters. Check the Secretary of State's website for guidelines about collecting forms and deadlines to have the forms submitted. Failure to handle these forms properly can be considered voter fraud.*

## Absentee ballots

It is critical that you understand how absentee ballots work in your area and how they can be a part of your campaign strategy. You should know the deadline to request a ballot, to send the ballot back, the reasons people are allowed to request them and who in your area typically requests them.

In some races, the margin of victory is within the number of absentee ballots that have been mailed in. Providing reminders, especially for elderly voters, can be extremely helpful.

# Get Out the Vote (GOTV)

For many of us campaign lovers, this is the most exciting, stressful, emotional day of the campaign. Our efforts during GOTV will determine if we wake up tomorrow with a loss or win.

The first thing you need to think about is where and when you're going to vote. Then you need to work with your Campaign Manager to determine what needs to be done on Election Day.

Are there people in your area who need rides to go vote?

Do you have a college campus in your area? How can you motivate them to go vote? Free pizza with an "I voted" sticker?

Who are the registered voters that don't vote regularly and could benefit from a friendly door knock by a volunteer?

You should know your vote number and your number one task on Election Day is to get as many people as possible out to vote and hope most them vote for you.

# THE CAMPAIGN

Yes, I saved this piece for last. Based on all the conversations that you have had with yourself and others leading to this point, you should have some ideas of what you want your campaign to look like. Oftentimes, people will plan the campaign without taking any of the previous factors into consideration.

Huge mistake.

You need to understand everything that happens around the campaign to create the campaign plan.

# Branding

This is huge and you will want to work with a marketing professional. Your brand is the visual representation of your campaign. Your brand package should include at least the following items:

→ Your campaign slogan – keep it short and catchy

→ Professional headshots - not pictures taken on your phone or someone else's phone but photos that are taken by a professional and edited to highlight your best features

→ Family photos - if you are not married, consider taking some photos with your parents, siblings, pets; people want to know that you are connected to someone

→ Colors - you don't have to stick with red, white and blue but you should have a color consultation to understand which feelings different colors and color combinations illicit before deciding

→ Campaign image - some people use their state, something that represents their area, or a text only design featuring their name and slogan. It doesn't matter what you use, if you use it consistently.

There are more elements that your Media team and/or Marketing Consultant will help you to develop but this is the starting point for you. Work with professionals to create your brand because it will ultimately become a part of history and your legacy.

# Look like a winner

Every time you leave the confines of your home, you need to look like a winner. People will be making instant judgements about your ability to lead and govern based on a two second glance at you in the grocery store.

Does that mean that you need to wear a suit and tie or a full face of makeup every time you leave home?

No!

In fact, it's quite the opposite. You need to consistently balance the fine line of looking like you care about your appearance – from a good haircut, manicure nails, unscuffed shoes to pressed clothes – with looking like a normal resident of the community. People want leaders that they can relate to daily. However, when you are scheduled for an appearance, they want to see you turn on your charm and work your magic. They want to know that you can do both. Either or is not an option.

You should consider having a signature item in your look. One Congresswoman always wears a hat and people look forward to seeing which hat she will have on at different events.

A Congressman is known for his cufflinks. He collects them from all over the world and people enjoy seeing the different designs and striking up conversations about his adventures.

Yours may be a style of shoe, a scarf, necktie or even signature color but having something that people can connect with creates conversation. Do not tell people to check out your signature item. It should be subtly emphasized by your media team.

# Using online tools

You may or may not be proficient with social media and/or technology but a campaign has so many moving parts until you need to use technology to operate efficiently and you need social media to exponentially expand your reach. Here are a few tools that your campaign should consider integrating into your campaign plan:

> **group text messaging** - there are several apps that allow you to create group messaging. These will be important to ensure your teams have immediate access to each other. Be strategic about the groups that you create and discourage private conversations from occurring in the group messaging as well as conversations about sensitive issues. Whenever possible, make it a habit to discuss sensitive issues in person.

➢ **Website** - your website should be designed before you announce your candidacy. Once you announce, people will begin looking for information about you. Your website is where you tell the story that you want people to know. If you don't have your story created, people will go to your Facebook, Twitter, Google and any other source to create a story about you. Don't give anyone that much control over your campaign's brand. The most important features on your website are your "donate" button and a form for visitors to sign up for additional information from the campaign.

- ➢ **Email database** - collect email addresses at every opportunity. Your email database will allow you to communicate directly with your donors, supporters, and voters. This tool is invaluable because you cannot control how often people visit your website or social media pages but you increase the likeliness that they will see your message when you are contacting them directly.

- ➢ **Facebook** - you may or may not have a good relationship with Facebook but it is a tool that you need to use for your campaign. You need a Facebook professional page. Do not use your personal page as your primary campaign page. A professional page will allow you to analyze the data around advertising, users and persons who like your page. It also allows you to schedule posts, connect with other pages, and promote videos/ads to audiences that you target.

➤ **Twitter** - what impact can 140 characters have on your campaign? I'm sure a recent presidential election can answer that question for you. No, your campaign, unless you are running for President, will not be that massive however you should not discount the power of building an online community through common interests, hashtags, and tweetable quotes.

➢ **Instagram** - people like looking at pictures. They look at pictures to judge you. No one else may ever tell you that but I am brave enough to say it. Most people will look at what you are wearing, your body language, the expression of the people around you, the background, and any other information that they can find to formulate opinions about you. With that in mind, make sure that every picture you post is a good representative of you and your campaign, even if you have to stage some of the pictures.

➢ **YouTube** - you may or may not be comfortable with video. I know the feeling if you are not but videos are another great tool to connect with your audience. When you post videos, you can speak directly to your audience. When making your videos, have something prepared to say so that you are not rambling, check your lighting, check your background, ensure you have good audio and control your body language.

# Direct Mail

Let me start with, direct mail is expensive. Depending on the size of your area, it can be extremely expensive. Take a second to calculate the postage on sending a mailer to every household in your area (households are a different calculation from voters because some households will contain multiple voters).

Therefore, you need to be strategic with your direct mail campaign. A few things to consider:

1. **Direct mail works.** People are visual and they like to touch stuff, even if they touch it and throw it away.

2. **Direct mail builds name recognition.** The pieces allow you into the homes and hands of your target market.

3. **Direct mail allows you to target your messages.** Based on the household demographics, you can determine which component of your platform will speak to those households as well as which images will resonant with them.

There are many, many other benefits that your Marketing Consultant can share with you. Even if you are on a tight budget, you should plan to send at least one persuasion mailing to the group that you are attempting to influence. If you have a larger budget, you can consider sending an introduction to your campaign, invitations to events, reminders for absentee voting, an early voting reminder and election day reminders.

Remember, direct mailing allows you to segment your list so that you don't have to send every mailing to every household. You can divide the lists into groups depending upon their demographics to determine which messages you want to communicate to them.

# Location

Campaign offices are rarely very fancy. Sad but true statement. In my experience, at the beginning stage of the campaign, they are usually small spaces being subleased from a seasonal business. Many campaigns do not invest a lot of money in the offices because they are temporary locations. Their primary purpose is to have a space for volunteers to come and assist with campaign related tasks like making signs, stuffing envelopes, assembling packs for door knocking and making phone calls to recruit volunteers and persuade voters. The office is also the ideal location for media interviews, preferably when you have excited volunteers performing meaningful tasks.

Allocate a small budget to decorating the space so that it looks lively and bright. If you are not creative or don't have time, delegate the task to a staffer or volunteer. Also, visit

Pinterest to get some ideas. Share those with the person who you are delegating to so that the office represents your personality.

# Messaging

You have done a self-assessment, thought about staff, volunteers, media, finances, branding, social media, and even whether you will have an office or not... now I must ask, **what is your message?**

I challenge you to focus your message on the issues that matter to the community and not focus solely on what you think is important. You may want to pull together some informal focus groups of people with diverse backgrounds to talk about the issues facing the community, how they believe your office can impact those issues, and what their expectations of your office are. If you see there is a disconnect, you may want to focus on education before persuasion.

Your messaging should flow naturally but it should in no way be off handed or off the cuff. Your stump speech will be long because it will be a summary of your entire platform.

However, the entire speech should not be given to every crowd.

Speak to the people you are speaking to. Elaborate on the issues that they are concerned about.

Does this make you disingenuous?

No, not if you are consistent. Don't take a different position on the issue. Choose your position or choose not to have a position and commit to investigating further but do not flip flop on the issue. Go deeper on the issues not broader.

# Fundraising

The final and possibly most important consideration is how you will fundraise.

Where will you get money?

There are many ways for you to raise money and you should ensure they are in line with your state's campaign finance laws. You also need to understand

- what disclosures should be provided to donors
- how much individuals can donate and within what time frame
- what financial records need to be kept
- which groups you can accept donations from and what amount
- what information you are required to collect and how long you need to keep it
- what information you need to provide to your state election commission

- what information you need to provide to the Federal Election Commission

It will be up to you and your staffers to determine how you will generate the funds. Whatever plan you create, make sure it is realistic and that you stick with it so that you can run the campaign that you believe will help you win the race.

At the end of Election Day, you need to feel confident that you did all you could every day of the race.

# About the Author

## LaKesha Womack

Growing up LaKesha imagined going to law school and becoming a United States Senator. She loves to gather the facts, formulate her opinion and participate in a good debate. Although she received a Bachelor's Degree in Political Science from Vanderbilt University, her love for fashion, finances and business took her down several other career paths which have ultimately led to her forming Womack Consulting Group. The small firm provides Political Strategy Consulting among its many other services. She is an alum of the Women's Campaign School at Yale University, an Official Member of the Forbes Coaches Council, a former Campaign Organizer and has served as an adviser and campaign manager to several campaigns.

LaKesha has found that she enjoys helping candidates find their voice, develop their strategy and cheer them through Election Day.

She is the published author of seven additional titles and enjoys traveling across the country as a keynote speaker, workshop facilitator and seminar presenter.

Contact LaKesha for a complimentary consultation to discuss your campaign or book LaKesha to speak at your upcoming event – WomackCG.com